GROOKS

PIET HEIN

GROOKS

BORGENS BILLIGBØGER 85

© Piet Hein 1966
Cover and illustrations: Piet Hein
2nd edition 13th printing 1994
Narayana Press, Gylling

628.500 copies of grook volumes in English
have now been printed

ISBN 87-418-1079-1

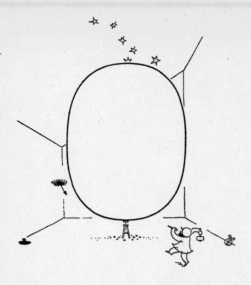

ARS BREVIS

There is
one art,
no more,
no less:
to do
all things
with art-
lessness.

PROBLEMS

Problems worthy
   of attack
prove their worth
   by hitting back.

THE ETERNAL TWINS

Taking fun
   as simply fun
and earnestness
   in earnest
shows how thoroughly
   thou none
of the two
   discernest.

CONSOLATION GROOK

Losing one glove
is certainly painful,
but nothing
    compared to the pain
of losing one,
throwing away the other,
and finding
    the first one again.

T. T. T.

Put up in a place
where it's easy to see
the cryptic admonishment
   T. T. T.

When you feel how depressingly
slowly you climb,
it's well to remember that
   Things Take Time.

OMNISCIENCE

Knowing what
thou knowest not
is in a sense
omniscience.

6

SIMPLY ASSISTING GOD

I am a humble artist
moulding my earthly clod,
adding my labour to nature's,
simply assisting God.

Not that my effort is needed;
yet somehow, I understand,
my maker has willed it that I too should have
unmoulded clay in my hand.

HINT AND SUGGESTION

Admonitory grook addressed to youth.

The human spirit sublimates
the impulses it thwarts;
a healthy sex life mitigates
the lust for other sports.

MANKIND

Men, said the Devil,
are good to their brothers:
they don't want to mend
their own ways, but each other's.

NAIVE –

Naive you are
if you believe
life favours those
who aren't naive.

THE MIRACLE OF SPRING

We glibly talk
   of nature's laws
but do things have
   a natural cause?

Black earth turned into
   yellow crocus
is undiluted
   hocus-pocus.

DREAM INTERPRETATION
Simplified.

Everything's either
concave or -vex,
so whatever you dream
will be something with sex.

PRAYER

to the sun above the clouds.

Sun that givest all things birth,
shine on everything on earth!

If that's too much to demand,
shine at least on this our land.

If even that's too much for thee,
shine at any rate on me.

CIRCUMSCRIPTURE

As Pastor X steps out of bed
    he slips a neat disguise on:
that halo round his priestly head
    is really his horizon.

SOCIAL MECHANISM

When people always
try to take
the very smallest
piece of cake
how can it also
always be
that that's the one
that's left for me?

A TOAST

The soul may be a mere pretence,
the mind makes very little sense.
So let us value the appeal
of that which we can taste and feel.

ON PROBLEMS

Our choicest plans
    have fallen through,
our airiest castles
    tumbled over,
because of lines
    we neatly drew
and later neatly
    stumbled over.

AN ETHICAL GROOK

I see
    and I hear
        and I speak no evil;
I carry
    no malice
        within my breast;
yet quite without
    wishing
        a man to the Devil
one may be
    permitted
        to hope for the best.

LILAC TIME

The lilacs are flowering, sweet and sublime,
     with a perfume that goes to the head;
and lovers meander in prose and rhyme,
trying to say –
          for the thousandth time –
     what's easier done than said.

THE DOUBLE-DOOR EFFECT

Double doors are justified
because they're comfortably wide.
Therefore you only half undo'em;
and therefore nothing can get through 'em.

FORETASTE WITH AFTERTASTE

Corinna's scanty evening dress
reveals her charms to an excess
which makes a fellow lust for less.

MAJORITY RULE

His party was the Brotherhood of Brothers,
and there were more of them than of the others.
That is, they constituted that minority
which formed the greater part of the majority.
Within the party, he was of the faction
that was supported by the greater fraction.
And in each group, within each group, he sought
the group that could command the most support.
The final group had finally elected
a triumvirate whom they all respected.
Now of these three, two had the final word,
because the two could overrule the third.
One of these two was relatively weak,
so one alone stood at the final peak.
He was: THE GREATER NUMBER of the pair
which formed the most part of the three that were
elected by the most of those whose boast
it was to represent the most of most
of most of most of the entire state –
or of the most of it at any rate.
He never gave himself a moment's slumber
but sought the welfare of the greatest number.
And all the people, everywhere they went,
knew to their cost exactly what it meant
to be dictated to by the majority.
But that meant nothing, – they were the minority.

EXPERTS

Experts have
their expert fun
ex cathedra
telling one
just how nothing
can be done.

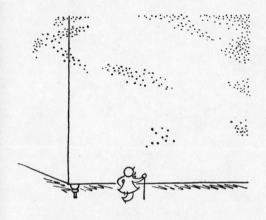

ATOMYRIADES

Nature, it seems, is the popular name
for milliards and milliards and milliards
of particles playing their infinite game
of billiards and billiards and billiards.

ROAD SENSE

God save us, now they're murdering
        another winding road,
and another lovely countryside
        will take another load
of pantechnicon and car and motorbike.
        They're busy making bigger roads,
        and better roads and more,
so that people can discover
        even faster than before
        that everything is everywhere alike.

OUR NOBLEST ACHIEVEMENT

We must expect posterity
to view with some asperity
    the marvels and the wonders
        we're passing on to it;
but it should change its attitude
to one of heartfelt gratitude
    when thinking of the blunders
        we didn't quite commit.

THE TRUE DEFENCE

The only defence
that is more than pretence
is to act on the fact
that there is no defence.

PAST PLUPERFECT

The past, – well, its just like
       our Great-Aunt Laura,
who cannot or will not perceive
that though she is welcome,
       and though we adore her,
yet now it is time to leave.

MY FAITH IN DOCTORS

My faith in doctors
        is immense.
Just one thing spoils it:
        their pretence
of authorised
        omniscience.

DEFENCE WANTED

In International
      Consequences
the players must reckon
      to reap what they've sown.
We have a defence
      against other defences,
but what's to defend us
      against our own?

GETTING DOWN TO FUNDAMENTALS

It will steadily shrink,
our earthly abode,
until antipode stands
upon antipode.

Then, soles together,
the planet gone,
we'll know the ground
that we rest upon.

GROOK TO STIMULATE GRATITUDE

in sour rationalists.

As things so
     very often are
intelligence
     won't get you far.

So be glad
     you've got more sense
than you've got
     intelligence.

MISSING LINK

Man's a kind
of Missing Link,
fondly thinking
he can think.

THE ROAD TO WISDOM

The road to wisdom? – Well, it's plain
and simple to express:
       Err
       and err
       and err again
       but less
       and less
       and less.

THAT IS THE QUESTION
Hamlet Anno Domini.

Co-existence
or no existence.

BRIDGE OR TUNNEL?
Channel project.

A tunnel would be possible,
    a bridge would also do,
but wouldn't it be better to
    amalgamate the two?

Let bridge and tunnel undulate
    in waves from shore to shore,
keeping green the memories
    of those who went before

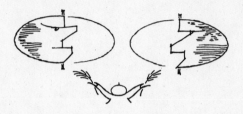

LOSING FACE

The noble art of losing face
may one day save the human race
        and turn into eternal merit
what weaker minds would call disgrace.

A PSYCHOLOGICAL TIP

Whenever you're called on to make up your mind,
  and you're hampered by not having any,
the best way to solve the dilemma, you'll find,
  is simply by spinning a penny.

No – not so that chance shall decide the affair
  while you're passively standing there moping;
but the moment the penny is up in the air,
  you suddenly know what you're hoping.

MORE HASTE –

Inscription for a monument at the crossroads.

Here lies, extinguished in his prime,
a victim of modernity:
but yesterday he hadn't time –
and now he has eternity.

A WORD TO THE WISE

Let the world pass in its time-ridden race;
    never get caught in its snare.
Remember, the only acceptable case
for being in any particular place
    is having no business there.

MEETING THE EYE

You'll probably find
      that it suits your book
to be a bit cleverer
      than you look.

Observe that the easiest
      method by far
is to look a bit stupider
      than you are.

IF YOU KNOW WHAT I MEAN

A poet should be of the
             old-fashioned meaningless brand:
obscure, esoteric, symbolic, –
             the critics demand it;
so if there's a poem of mine
             that you do understand
I'll gladly explain what it means
             till you don't understand it.

THE CASE FOR OBSCURITY

On Thoughts and Words I.

If no thought
your mind does visit,
make your speech
not too explicit.

LEST FOOLS SHOULD FAIL

True wisdom knows
it must comprise
some nonsense
as a compromise,
lest fools should fail
to find it wise.

GROOK ON LONG-WINDED AUTHORS

Long-winded writers I abhor,
    and glib, prolific chatters;
give me the ones who tear and gnaw
    their hair and pens to tatters:
who find their writing such a chore
    they only write what matters.

OUT OF TIME

A holiday thought.

My old clock used to tell the time
 and subdivide diurnity;
but now it's lost both hands and chime
 and only tells eternity.

AN ODE TO MODESTY

Talking of successful rackets
modesty deserves a mention.
Exclamation marks in brackets
never fail to draw attention.

THE CURE FOR EXHAUSTION

Sometimes, exhausted
with toil and endeavour,
I wish I could sleep
for ever and ever;
but then this reflection
my longing allays:
I shall be doing it
one of these days.

I'D LIKE –

I'd like to know
what this whole show
is all about
before it's out.

A MAXIM FOR VIKINGS

Here is a fact
  that should help you to fight
  a bit longer:

Things that don't act-
  ually kill you outright
  make you stronger.

MAKING SENSE

Life makes sense
and who could doubt it,
if we have
no doubt about it.

A MOMENT'S THOUGHT

As eternity
is reckoned
there's a lifetime
in a second.

LIVING IS –

Living is
   a thing you do
now or never –
   which do you?

THE END

TITLE INDEX

FIRST LINE INDEX